In My Own Words

By Shirley Taylor

Shirley's first book to be published was titled
"Chon-Toh-gnah-kah"

littleauthors.shop
Copyright © 2021 Shirley Taylor
ISBN: 9781952330155

All rights reserved. No part of this publication may be reproduced, distributed, or transmitted in any form or by any means, including photocopying, recording, or other electronic or mechanical methods, without the prior writtten permission of the author.

Dedicated to...

Three Angels in my life:

Brent Johnston
G.W. Hardin
Matt O'Brien

Without them this book would not have been possible.

Contents

Part One--Poems

Obscurity	10
A Bird's Song	11
The Hummingbird	12
Where Are You?	13
Dreams/Visions	14
A Wildflower	15
Who Am I?	16
The Ones Before Me	17
Love in My Heart	18
Raindrops	19
God's Heart	20
Wind	21
Sand	22
What Makes Water Blue?	23
Fighting the Unseen	24
Traveling	25
I Paint	26
How Can I Choose?	27
A Note	28
Follow Through	29
We Were Here	30
Rejection	31
What Are You Made Of?	32
Immortality	33
Yuletide	34
The Summons	35
Thought	36
Bruises	37
My Dwelling	38
Technology	39
Nature of Art	40
Public Conversion	41
Birth of a Child	42
Please Help	43
Prayer/Meditation	44

Do I Believe?	45
What Type of Bug?	46
Destined to Leave	47
De'ja Vu	48
No Death	49
Little Things Are Seen	50
What is Real	51
Why Me?	52
Nature's Building Blocks	53
Past - Present - Future	54
Signs of Spring	55
Communication	56
Never Still	57
Television	58
Power of One	59

Part Two--Thoughts to Ponder

Wounds of the Heart	62
How Much Do Things Cost?	62
Your Best Defense	62
Inside - Out	62
A Sharp Tongue	62
Spicy Secrets	62
How Big	63
Atoms and Missiles	63
A Good Investment	63
Two Year Olds	63
A Tree	63
Eagerness to Learn	63
Wood and Atoms	64
Free-Form	64
Leaves Falling	64
Growing Things	64
Beauty in All	64
Building Trust	64
End Result	65
The Family Parrot	65
Length	65
Control Your Speed	65

Tunnels	65
New Vision	65
The Traveling	66
A Ribbon of Light	66
Concentration	66
A Good Laugh	66
Staying Close	66
A Driving Force	66
Man Without God	67
Still Enough	67
Forgiveness	67
Telling a lie	67
Rain / Loved One	67
Problem Solving	68
Road Construction	68
A Helping Hand	68
Patience	68
The Divine Radio	68
Clearing Out	68
What Do You Expect?	68
Centers of Intelligence	68
Strong/Weak	69
Silence and Hidden Mystery	69
A Silent Voice	69
Remain Childlike	69
Hide and Seek	70
Reason I Flunked	70
The Correct Number	70
Be Present	70
Learning to Focus	70
Widen/Loosen	70
Accept the Unreality	71
Self - Sufficient	71
Second Chance	71
Love Lives Forever	71
Within and Within	71
Unfolding	71
Fullness of Grace	72
Conduct	72
One and the Same	72

Hay	72
Thoughts	72
Footprints	72
Precious Stones	73
Good Friends Good Wine	73
A Garden	73
Wise and Solemn	73
Rule Number One	73
Honesty	73
Natural Birthright	74
By Example	74
Sunflowers	74
Psyche	74
True Followers	74
Four Words	74
We Do Things	75
Seeing The World	75
Three Areas	75
Expectation or Realization?	75
The Rose Window	76
Masquerading	76
Always A Choice	76
Have Time	76
Shade - Relief - Comfort	76

Part Three--Short Essays

Loving Fully	80
I'm Sorry - Just Two Words	81
Ten Questions	82
Gift Giving	83
Want/Need	84
Love	85
Sound Travel	86
When Will We See	87
A Few Gentle Moments	88
Seven Challenges	90
Three Stages	91

Part One

Poems

Obscurity

When mist is in the air
Uncertainty reigns close.

As the vapors surround me
Moisture permeates my soul.

I feel a coolness within,
Heart rate slows down to a crawl.

As the maker pulls strings
Gentle tugs reach the haze.

Have I been unaware?
Have I been taut and dense?

Answers lie covered in dew,
Heat rising, warming the fog.

Progression is beginning
I have a "lone" way to go.

Decrease before increase,
Law of Supreme Being.

A Bird's Song

Hearing a bird sing is like receiving
a drop of Christ's blood.

Beyond understanding,
yet surrounded with Agape love.

The eyes widen. . .
Heart rate increases. . .
Abundant joy filling my heart. . .

The Hummingbird

Smallest of birds
Greatness of will. . .

Tic-tac size eggs
The nest they fill. . .

Flitting about
Never alighting. . .

Wings beating wildly
Sometimes miss a-sighting. . .

Tending the young
A full-time job. . .

Being a loner
Called often a snob. . .

Prince of the sky
Title well won. . .

Watching in awe
Their work, well done.

Where Are You?

Where are you my darling,
Can't see your face?
Are you peaceful and happy
In your new place?

Is grass green, do birds sing
What about trees?
What one does affects all
Even the bees.

Is Heaven a real place
Or a state of mind?
Is "now" like "forever"
One of a kind?

I have lots of questions
As you can see,
The answers lie hidden,
Am I still me?

Dreams/Visions

Is it chimera or observation?
Is it reverie or witnessing?

Is getting a glimpse of another
Dimension a vision?
Does a dream show insight or imagination?

As I leave my body and fly to another destination,
Am I experiencing a vision
Or looking into a new reality,
Or is it an illusion of make-belief?

Many types, many explanations,
It boggles my mind.
I surmise we accept what applies
To our own self,
Leaving the rest in the arms of the experts.

You are your own best teacher.
Trust inside of you.

A Wildflower

What am I, but a song,
A poem formed by God.
Observed by Deity
The sun gives a nod.

Unseen, like God I live
To lose myself, be free.
Release pursuits of life,
I only need to "Be."

Who Am I?

I used to be yellow
Now I am white.
Color does not matter,
I'm puffy and bright.

When the wind blows I'm ready
To go up and away
I'll have new adventures
Scattering seed each new day.

Some folks call me trashy
A word I don't relish,
We all have our beauty
Even dandelions we cherish.

The Ones Before Me

What is reincarnation?
How does it affect me?
It depends on the wisdom
Of the ones I now be.

The living ones before me
Are playing a huge part
Of the life I'm now living,
Hiding deep in my heart.

They influence the choices
Of my everyday life,
I wonder, can they hear me
As I stumble through strife?

There are so many voices
I can hear them at night,
Each one teaching me lessons
When my soul is in flight.

If I listen through daytime
If my mind is aware
If I'm open and willing
Those before me will care.

Love in My Heart

Love in my heart is God's
    Love for God.

Love in my heart is God's
    Love for man.

Understanding this love gives
    Peace to my spirit
To my inner self
To the very core of my being.

Raindrops

Drops of water falling from the clouds
Descending quantity or quality?
Is there considerable amount
Or simply a degree of excellence?

The answer depends on contact point,
Looking through glass, a downpour of water,
Elijah's magic, the Grace of God,
The spiritual influence of Heaven.

Sometimes drops filter inside my heart.
They remind me of tears unable to fall.
Water drizzling down on the panes,
Tiny droplets let loose; my heart expands.

Patter of rain on the roof denotes joy.
I have opened myself up to Love.
Like the "Louvre" desires peace and quiet
I receive understanding and grace.

The tears of God are rain coming down.
The freedom I feel envelopes my all.
Tears unable to fall are no more
As evolution of Love is my guide.

God's Heart

I saw God's heart today
Tulip tree bud opened up.
Tiny flecks of color showing
From the center of the magical cup.

I stood there unable to move
My eyes glued to the process in view.
It's not often we see into God
With His wonders appearing as new.

The bud is there for us all
Just a glance is what it takes,
Too busy, unfocused to look
Mind wanders to sand, beach and lakes.

So glad I walked quietly by
And was able to see in God's Heart
I feel born anew in His eyes
Thanking Nature herself for this Art.

Wind

Movement of air, a current, an aura adrift,
What is this ventilation refreshing mankind?
A gust, blast or flurry perhaps puff, whiff or blow,
They all send streams of air and a catch of one's breath.

What are the makings of this diving known as wind?
No formulas invented by the wisest of souls,
There must be an answer if scientists have their way.
Technology does have its limits, even today.

What has happened to mystery? It's now out of date.
Do we have to know answers to all heavenly things?
I'm happy just living in awareness and peace.
Let me inhale and exhale capfuls of air. . . lest it cease.

Sand

I press my toes in loose particles of hard broken rock.
I love the beach. It is my place of peace.

A flat circular sea urchin washes close to my foot.
Where have you been? What stories can you tell?

My first sand dollar of the season, what a charming find.
Who else will come calling? Refinement is near.

The specks of tiny granules squish up and over both feet.
They sparkle and glisten as sun zeros down.

What magic is hiding in these grains of beach desert sand?
Could I hold this moment of wedded bliss?

Let go, become free of what is coarse or uncouth.
The lesson sand taught me. . . "Finding My Truth."

What Makes Water Blue?

Protons filter through the water.
Color red is first to dissolve.

Orange, yellow and green, not strong enough to survive.
What will blue do? It's next in line.

Red color becomes rust as it fades in the deep.
Azure and sapphire come into view.

They hold protons at bay for a time
And then there is darkness abound.

Indigo is the reason why water "looks" blue.
I'm trusting "my toughness" will see me through.

Fighting the Unseen

"Don't have money for my child's surgery needs."
Those 11 syllables cut into my soul.
A mother should never have to say those words.
Will this virus ever end taking its toll?
"Fighting the Unseen"

They'll have to stay with their Father.
Don't know what else now I can say.
Our salon may be shutting doors,
What will I do to find my way?
"Fighting the Unseen"

Cutting hair, helping people is what I know,
Never been so unsettled in all my life.
It's like fighting a battle I cannot win,
Cutting me to pieces with a sharp, sharp knife.
"Fighting the Unseen"

Who should I pray to? Where shall I go?
My life is unsettled right now.
My rent's due tomorrow, I know.
To the Angels of God, I now bow.
"Fighting the Unseen"

Traveling

How do you travel? How do I?
Is your life an expedition?
Or do you wander aimlessly?

As I look back over the years,
Walk, ride, explore. . . tourist - all four.
Finding my way, I tread in place.

Always taking the safer route,
Confidence in self, short supply,
Decades of journeys, travel stained.

The grand tour of life almost done,
The road map of travel worn out.
Memories and keepsakes take wing.
Traveling. . .

I Paint

Do I sketch, compose or simply copy?
Whatever the genre, I paint.

Picking up the brush, my heart skips a beat,
A challenge before me, now lives.

The darks go in first as they are the base,
The rest, a tableau to arrange.

Realism, Pop-Art, whatever the style,
Happy thoughts to me from the start.

I paint to give others a point of view,
I paint for myself to depict.

The finished picture gives me peace within,
What joy to my life this has been.

How Can I Choose?

Art, music, writing, the joys of my life.
Which one to choose, I cannot.

All three are equal in my mind's eye
Giving tranquil calmness and peace.

Author, painter, teacher of the scale
Matters not which class I embrace.

They're in my life's blood, streaming to my soul
Like breath of a flame within.

Thank you, God, for giving me these gifts,
Without them I'd mold -- not lift.

28
A Note

Could be a letter, memo, tone or sound
Depends on your frame of evidence. . .

It gets my attention, be very sure
Is it writing or notation. . .?

Simple little word "note" - what is the source?
Round with a stem or a missive . . .?

I've come across both in my time on earth
One to remind, other speaks tone. . .

Could be the same, both give prompts, hints and cues,
Information of origin, the key. . .

Follow Through

Are the words sincere?
The talker believes so.

His intention a pledge,
Or just a desire?

Easy to decide,
Wait for follow through.

If none comes then you'll know,
Utterance was bogus.

We Were Here

We once lived. Now we are gone.
We were born. We lived. We died.
The circle continues on.

So many walked on the earth.
They breathed, existing in the flesh
Like grains of sand on the beach.

Now they too have faded out,
Lifetimes washed away unnoticed.
No one remembers.
"We Were Here."

Our height, weight, color of eyes,
Our desires, loves and passions,
We are gravestones sunk in water.

So why do we become authors, paint pictures, compose music?
Maybe one future child will perceive.
They will behold, observe and take note,
A seed of remembrance, planted.
Descendants comprehend that
"We Were Here."

Rejection

Nothing worse than rejection,
Withholding love, refused care.
I cannot survive rebuffed.
I simply exist, not thrive.

What causes one to dismiss?
Why did they lay me aside?
Do my cries fall on deaf ears?
What have "I done" to cause fears?

Living this way for affection,
I'm learning why discard took place.
I'm sorry for those who repel,
For they are the ones who lose face.

They live their years full of sorrow
Regretting the choices they've made.
Jealous thoughts form, actions then swarm.
It's best to forgive. . . Karma fades.

What Are You Made Of?

Do you like hanging on to something?
Are you afraid to let go?
Why do you keep something if it is not pleasing to you?
How long are you going to be upset over events in the past?
Just exactly what are you made of anyway?

>Are you living in the past?
>Are you living in the future?
>Are you living the present moment of now?

The Choice Is Yours.

Immortality

Children, descendants, kindred tribes,
Through them comes immortality.
Hold in esteem or non-binding?
All depends on belief and aim.

Some want names only for records,
Making sure their creed is fulfilled.
Several wish to know their families.
Nomenclature to them is real.

What is your vision of family?
Appreciate or simply find names?
Unless we acquire for wisdom
Then Love has no home in the games.

As parents teach their children. . .
So their children teach children. . .
Their children teach children. . .
Thus immortality reigns.

Yuletide

Christmas is a type of Hades for those
      who have lost someone dear.
Should be a joyful celebration
      Instead the day lacking cheer.

I'm aware of pandemic and need,
      Still there's a loss of loved one not here.
Passage of time - not an option
      Wanting to hold them close with no tear.

For a moment I pause breathing
      Watching scenes the yuletide brings.
Knowing someday we'll be together,
      Listen close. . . flutter of Angel wings.

The Summons

Daughter summons Mom to spend
    Afternoon with her.

Trust Mom appreciates this chance
    Of fate to occur.

A ride with laughter lunch and love
    Between the two.

Been waiting years for a call,
    Days left now are few.

Summary

Daughter chooses Mom. . .
Magnificent Day. . .
Vigilant Waiting. . .
No summons my way. . .

Thought

Reflection, speculation,
Ideas flow, pondering,
Or is it resolution
Without deliberation?

Do you determine outcome
Before self-consultation?
Does thoughtfulness play a part
Or is judgment a certainty?

A thought becomes "an act" if voiced.
Utterance expressed makes it "real".
Better to think before speaking.
To muse before speech is "ideal."

Bruises

I bruise so easily these days,
A bump, blood test, or IV.
Tiny veins and scar tissue reigns,
No solution in sight do I see.

A black and blue spot appears.
Wondering how long it will stay?
Some last a week, some three or four.
I wish they would last just a day.

Sometimes a bruise can't be seen.
It hides deep inside our hearts.
It simmers and boils deep inside,
Unable to halt once it starts.

Tears flow like wine from the eyes,
Emotions both bitter and sweet.
It's not my fault, no guilt I see
Understanding the source I now greet.

Bruised both real and unseen,
Both contusion spots I fear.
Intense and telling they glow,
A blot to extinguish -- not smear.

My Dwelling

My dwelling is not alive if I am not alive
With everything inside her walls.

Walking through rooms looking at treasures I have idolized makes me realize an important truth.

If a collection owns you, it is just a group of possessions symbolizing unfulfilled dreams.
I have now stopped enshrining them.

I now simply rejoice "with" my belongings.
I do not want more things to exist amongst.
I have heart attachment to my acquisitions.
I enjoy their company.
I experience them.
I am alive with them.

My dwelling is not alive if I am not alive inside her walls.

Technology

Does technology suppress creativity?
If reference concerns nature and art, could be true.

Putting affirmation on seat of thought
Excludes technical methods.

One needs the imagination of expression
To suggest and create.

Technology has its place in instrumentality.
Do not confuse this with nature and art and life.

Nature of Art

Art is both a creation and
    Manifestation of the Divine.

It is an amplification of the
    Celestial inspired.

The one who brings a thing into a
    "Living being" borders on esoteric thought.

The result of the creation can be
    Specific or metaphysical in structure.

Both depict the innermost temple
    Of essence.

Therefore; the task of an onlooker is the discovery of this completion of awareness of "his own being" and the "object observed" as One.

This is the nature of Art.

Public Conversion

Christ came as the Word.
The Word is not heard.
State of personage denied.
Power rejects those who cried.

All human life reflects God.
Black versus white hails a nod.
Christ's voice today is bleak.
Christians sometimes condemn as they speak.

Let your actions speak loud and clear.
The image of God should not fear.
Racism is built into us.
Don't let our minds become pus.

Public conversion must reign
In order to keep our world sane.

Birth of a Child

Pain filled with beauty,
    How can this be?
      "The
          Birth
              Of
                  A
                      Child"

God sees the anguish of blood, sweat and tears.
      "The
          Birth
              Of
                  A
                      Child"

Wonder of wonders, bliss fills the heart.
      "The
          Birth
              Of
                  A
                      Child"

Please Help

My friend is anxious.
Please quiet her fears.
Fill the mind with peace
Even through her tears.

Her soul is gentle
And so full of Love.
Lots of living to do
With help from above.

Thank you, God, for listening
To my plea for Dear Bea.
She deserves the best.
Please set her heart free.

Prayer/Meditation

"Ask --
     Solicit --
          Eulogize --
               Glorify" --

"Listen --
     Ponder --
          Contemplate --
               Trust" --

Understanding the difference,
Communion with Yahweh,
Trust in expectation,
Embrace the unknown.

All
     I
          Need

              For
                   Wisdom.

Do I Believe?

Blood shed. . .
Agony abounds. . .
Absolving sin. . .
    Do I believe?

Appearance displayed. . .
Quantity doubt. . .
Caress me not. . .
    Do I believe?

Centuries Pass. . .
Centuries Pass. . .
Centuries Pass. . .
    Still asking
    Do I believe?

46
What Type of Bug?

If you suffer with hives,

If you bite your fingernails,

If you have the insistence of always being right,

Perhaps the next step would be to figure out what type of bug is biting you?

Destined to Leave

Loving unreserved needs effort.
Simple affection is not enough.
When in the womb I kicked with anger.
Never felt at ease in your skin.

Are mortals destined to leave me?
Have I programmed this into my psyche?
Life has been a series of leavings.
Multitudes of those I've embraced are gone.

I've had to learn to live apart.
With my thoughts, dreams and inspirations.
Looming now before me, parting alone
Is the course I understand best.

This is what we all do at the time.

Manage. . .
    Complete. . .
        Close. . .
            Exit with Grace. . .

De'ja Vu

Have you ever experienced
    A memory?
        A vision?
            A reverie?
                Something already seen?

If so you have encountered de'ja vu.

Is de'ja vu a genuine existence?
It depends on the presumption of the recipient.

What you deem as your truth
    may not be my gospel.
Let's not be hasty in determining
    Another's connection.

Let the judgment be "His" and "His" alone.

No Death

As long as a name remains in your heart
And is spoken aloud there is not death.

There is no line between earth, sea and sky.
Why do we say, the sea ends, sky starts, and earth stands still?

There is no difference between them.
They blend together in a haze. . . no beginning - no end.

The universe is born with the dawning of each new day.

Names blazoned on the lips will never die.
Rebirth occurs with sunrise as its promise.

Little Things Are Seen

A droopy bunch of dandelions
    Held tight in a sweaty fist,
A mother's heart is happier
    With a loving hug and kiss.

A heaping platter of cookies
    And a friendly smile or nod,
A secret prayer for those you love
    And a silent talk with God.

A helping hand to friends in need
    As we walk along life's way,
A kiss to help the little hurts
    As they come along the way.

Maybe you think your talents
    Are few and far between
But "He" looks down with tenderness
    And each little thing is seen.

What is Real

I know I've lived before,
Don't know exactly "when."
It really doesn't matter,
It's as real now as "then."

I think about my past lives,
There were lessons to be "learned."
I pray Dear God in heaven
That this existence is well "earned."

The realness is inside me,
I feel it every "day."
I know the truth of God's word,
What more is there to "say?"

Why Me?

I am bringing you through fire,
I am bringing you through flame,
I am bringing you through windstorms,
I am bringing you through rain -

So your eyes may see the glory,
So your eyes may see the pain,
I am teaching you, my servant
To be reverent, not profane -

For you will be my teacher,
Yes, you will show my plan,
To all of those around you
Who long to know the "Son of Man."

Nature's Building Blocks

Can there be connections
      Across space - "time?"
If everything is located in space,
      The items are related as in faces of "mime."

Nature's building blocks mirror each "other."
      Is this illusion or is it all real?
Items have properties of relation as "brother."

Think about things as they actually "are."
      Looking at substance shows reaction of other,
Nature's building blocks are like specks of a "star."

54
Past - Present - Future

Traveling along the freeway I looked up to see an overpass just ahead with a long line of cattle passing over.

The cowboys were neatly positioned at both ends. Here was a glimpse of our country's <u>Past</u>.

We were traveling in a beautiful, air-conditioned car of the <u>Present</u>.

In the sky jets were exceeding the sound barrier, showing me the <u>Future</u>.

Funny how we are able to see three seasons of life, all in one glance.

Signs of Spring

Looking into the thicket I see
Some dark grey color still in view,
Lighter blue-grey also is showing through,
Grove still absent of any green,
Won't be long till some will be seen.

Looking carefully at the trees I see
Branches with sprouting buds being refined
Eager to burst out of stifling confine.
Even a hint of green I see,
Soon leaves will appear on every tree.

Looking up at Father Sky I see
Blankets of clouds hiding shades of blue
And behind the clouds, sunbeams shine for you.
It matters not if it's rainy and grey
Each hour of Spring, special in its own way.

Communication

Let go of what is absent
Place only realness before my eyes.
I must be fully present for
God to give himself to me. . .
And I to Him.

I must not force myself on God.
My own desires and activities be stilled.
Psalms in "Your Word" speak loud.
Forgive me for not paying homage to them.

If I am confused and full of fear,
He will not hear me.
Return to the present.
Be available in silence.
God has his way of communication.

Never Still

Our bodies not set in stone,
Constant movement within.
Blood streams through artery and vein,
Ideas reach the mind.

Even in sleep there is act,
Intellect always awake.
Surges of thought taking hold
Remembrance is the key.

No movement comes only in death,
Till then, activity reigns.
Remain calm, moments of fear pass.
"Breath Deep" through stages of life.

Television

TV is a blessing or could be a curse,
All depends on point of view.

There used to be programs of laughter and mirth, violence and sex
now the key.

Ungentle games and brute force numbing the mind,
Where now is moderation?

I may be old fashioned, not "in" with the crowd.
My awareness now is clear.

Self-restraint, self-control are words we don't use.
How sad for the young today.

A blessing of learning to those in the know,
A curse to those who don't care.

What would Farnsworth do? He invented TV.
I'm sure he'd feel both joy and pain.

Power of One

I am unsettled these days,
Disturbed by myths and untruths.
Our earth feels empty and void,
We are blind to lies being told.

Money, power, and greed abound,
Benevolence seems nonexistent.
Movements evade the problem,
Details and policies reign.

Answers now are to destroy,
Being humane, a mirage.
Psychology of Leaders in question,
Pride of technology boasting,

A change within is the answer,
Quietness, listening, and prayer.
Speak aloud when I'm able,
Fighting until no longer I breathe…

    This
            Is
                  The
                        "Power of One"

Part Two

Thoughts to Ponder

Wounds of the Heart

No wound of the heart ever heals.
It simply gets patched up to the point of functioning again.

How Much Do Things Cost?

The things that bring us absolute pleasure and happiness cost nothing -- So why do we owe the plastic card companies so much?

Your Best Defense

If a gloomy depressed person enters your home, he brings with him an aura of heaviness. Your best defense is to keep the negative thoughts from invading your precious space.

Inside - Out

The best things always come from the inside-out.

A Sharp Tongue

A woman's sharp tongue is rather like a saw that cuts and finally pierces the heart of a living tree.

Spicy Secrets

Everyone loves to be trusted with a spicy secret. They feel so important while telling it to someone.

How Big

How big a person is depends not on how much he eats, but how much gets under his skin.

Atoms and Missiles

All of the missiles and bombs built for peace is rather like expecting fire-crackers to keep silent.

A Good Investment

A few extra cemetery plots would be a good investment for all of us; for there-in we could keep the faults of our friends, family, and neighbors.

Two Year Olds

Two-year olds outside are like bottled pop. If you're not careful while capping, it will fizz and run in all directions.

A Tree

Whether great or small, a tree possesses certain stately qualities that no other living thing is capable of.

Eagerness to Learn

Most people are eager to learn, however, they are reluctant to the idea of being taught.

Wood and Atoms

If we could go back to the basics of splitting wood, maybe we wouldn't be so concerned about splitting atoms.

Free-Form

Do not ever completely aim for perfection. Nature is never perfect. She is an individual with free-form.

Leaves Falling

When leaves gently fall from trees, it is a whisper to man that life is an ever-changing process.

Growing Things

Most growing things will ripen in time if they are given tender-loving care.

Beauty in All

All of God's flowers have some beauty to them. Why must we be so eager to search out their faults.

Building Trust

A person who builds his trust and love around just one individual or train of thought is rather like a bee trying to gather all of his pollen from one flower.

End Result

Jumping across muddy places prevents you from getting dirty. Climbing ladders gets you to the top. What happens when you pluck the strings of your heart?

The Family Parrot

The parrot repeats all he hears. Be sure and live the kind of life you wouldn't be ashamed to let Polly hear all the details.

Length

Pairs of shorts come in all lengths -
So do haircuts -
So do skirts -
Length seems to be important in our life decisions.

Control Your Speed

When riding a bicycle downhill, it's hard to put on the brakes as you round the corner. Better learn to control your speed before you decide to make any turn.

Tunnels

Tunnels, elevators! Oh, how I hate closed-in places. There are so many avenues to explore. Take off the blinders before it's too late.

New Vision

Peeling the cataracts off of our eyes gives us new vision. Some of us never have this surgery performed, physically or spiritually.

The Traveling

Following your dreams is like seeing a rainbow. Your eyes never exactly come to the end - but the traveling is the most beautiful part.

A Ribbon of Light

Peace that transcends time is clear and pure. God is personal and part of me. I feel strength surrounding me as a ribbon of light.

Concentration

Many of us center our thoughts on the very things we wish to avoid. . . sickness, failure, and "what if?" It would be better to concentrate in our "God-mind" as we would get more satisfying results.

A Good Laugh

The only thing that gives the soul more pleasure than a smile is a good hearty laugh.

Staying Close

A true friend is rather like a watchful parent. He stays close by in case he is needed.

A Driving Force

"Being" an instrument of peace and light will evangelize our lives long before we "say" one word.

Man Without God

Man without God is like a heart without Love -
An eye unable to see -
A fragrance unable to be smelled -
And a lung without air.
How can we live without these things?

Still Enough

Do we talk a lot to cover our own inadequacy? Do we talk because we like to hear ourselves speak?
Maybe it's a little of both but remember: Only in silence can one really hear the answers to the most complex problems. We have to be still enough to listen.

Forgiveness

If everyone would forgive, there wouldn't be anything bad to forget.

Telling a lie

Telling a lie is like a giant sunflower swaying to and fro. When the wind blows, the seeds are scattered hither and yon.

Rain / Loved One

Don't ever worry or be upset if it rains on the day of the funeral of a loved one. God only weeps when one of His special spirits is called home.

Problem Solving

The amount of importance a person places on a thing determines his ability to solve that problem. Heavens, what a thought! I sure hope you place a great deal of importance on the problem of peace in the world today.

Road Construction

We passed a lot of construction on the road today. As far as I can tell, the only road that is in no need of repair is the straight and narrow.

A Helping Hand

The only place you can really find a helping hand is to realize it is attached to your own arm.

Patience

Dear Lord, I need to learn patience so desperately, but "please'" don't send anymore situations to teach me this blessed virtue.

The Divine Radio

The divine radio is always plugged in and in tune. If we do not make contact, it's our fault.

Clearing Out

In order for an empty vessel to be filled, a clearing out of former debris must occur. Only then can a fresh start happen.

What Do You Expect?

If you expect trouble and disappointment -
You get it.
If you expect pain -
you get it.
If you expect defeat -
You get it
Try expecting success and see what happens!

Centers of Intelligence

Pure centers of intelligence never die. They send out accomplishments to the atmosphere of the earth. Are you listening for divine instructions?

Strong/Weak

People who believe that strength and power are the seat of wisdom do not realize that true wisdom only comes to those who have understanding and become weak. . . Blessed are they.

Silence and Hidden Mystery

Only when outside voices can be quieted can the soul reflect on the hidden mystery of God. This can only be accomplished in silence.

A Silent Voice

A woman's eyes are her silent voice.

Remain Childlike

If I can remain childlike, I have a chance to be great. If not, I will tend to think I am great and remain small.

Hide and Seek

Remember the game hide and seek? Why did I always get caught? Suppose maybe I was being taught a lesson?

Reason I Flunked

I'm glad I learned the functions of left-brain, right-brain. Now I know why I always flunked Math!

The Correct Number

God gave us the absolute correct number of openings in our heads - two ears, two eyes, one nose, and one mouth. One is always better off if he keeps his eyes open and his ears listening; rather than sniffing around and doing all the talking.

Be Present

Wake up! Be aware!
Do not preach and lecture.
Simply be present and let each disciple either see or not see.

Learning to Focus

We should learn to focus on experiences, not so much on explanations. Let it be.

Widen/Loosen

To widen my understanding, I must loosen my grip; for only then do I work from the outside to the center.

Accept the Unreality

Before we can accept the unreality of things, we must first realize the reality of them.

Self - Sufficient

We try to teach our children to be self-sufficient, then our mother instincts surface and we realize we haven't let them know the meaning of denial.

Second Chance

The old woman muttered, 'I ain't done so good but I'm still all right. I ain't afraid to die. We all deserve a second chance.

Love Lives Forever
Love does not die. It is stronger than death. No religion or philosophy shall prevent me from rejoining the souls that I love.

Within and Within

Freedom is living peacefully within. It is not an escape.
The Spirit is within
And within
And within.

Unfolding

My own unfolding is coming from within like the bud of a flower opening to full bloom.

Fullness of Grace

The fullness of Grace is God's job and is completed by God. . .
Wait a minute. Is it my work too?

Conduct

Are you getting old when you start to complain of the younger generation's conduct? After all, who set the example?

One and the Same

If you are a good wife, you would be a good father. If you are a good husband, you would be a good mother. The roles are reversible.

Hay

While smelling hay, it all depends on your point of view. Are you lovers or are you a horse?

Thoughts

"Whatever thoughts you store in your mind will eventually make their way through your mouth."

Footprints

Too bad our thoughts can't leave footprints to show where we've been - like tracks in the snow.

Precious Stones

All of God's rocks are beautifully polished pebbles in the rough. Too bad we can't think of ourselves as God's precious stones.

Good Friends Good Wine

Good friends should enjoy each other like good wine. Both take an aging period.

A Garden

When one is cultivating and tending a garden, he is in close communion with the Creator.

Wise and Solemn

Even the wisest and most solemn in the world appreciate a little gaiety now and then. That's what makes them wise and solemn.

Rule Number One

We only become close when we let go of the need to control.

Honesty

Total honesty with another is being able to say what hurts, what feels good, and what we need.

Natural Birthright

We as human beings are born with the right to be happy. Why do we let someone come into our lives and ruin our natural birthright?

By Example

Do you repress your feelings? Children learn by example you know.

Sunflowers

Do you follow the dark of night or the light of the sun? I believe sunflowers have the answer.

Psyche

Did you know the word psyche in Greek means butterfly or soul? What a beautiful thing to ponder.

True Followers

True followers of a religious creed
Reject anything that undermines their persuasions.
Is this you?

Four Words

Belief and knowledge are two different things--
Just as hope and faith.
Don't believe me?
Look up these four words to validate.

We Do Things

Sometimes we do to our children the thing that was done to us, without realizing the consequences.

Seeing The World

Question:
Do we want young people through education to see the world through the eyes of the octogenarian generation?
Answer:
Yes? No? Both answers have merit.

Three Areas

Anger, boredom and discontent are harder to find a cure for than shooting off missiles, rockets and bombs. Why can't we address the most important issues of life instead of developing methods of destroying it?

Expectation or Realization?

Rose bushes either have young buds full of excitement at the possibility of bursting forth in full bloom, OR. . .
they have middle-age blossoms desperately hanging on to the young-bud beauty they once enjoyed.
Into which category do you belong? Each one has its own fulfillment.
Expectation or Realization?

The Rose Window

If you have ever visited "Chartres", a cathedral in Paris, you will never forget the diffused light that shines through the magnificent rose window, spreading peace and tranquility throughout this beautiful edifice.
If I could bottle this feeling of peace it would sell for an undetermined amount. Better yet, give it away to all who wish to experience this unconditional feeling of Love.

Masquerading

Does the older generation simply masquerade their own disappointments in life? I wonder?

Always A Choice

Is there ever a choice between fate and free will? Have we always tried to fix the problems of others? Why not try and fix a few of our own?
There is always a choice.

Have Time

When people say they don't have time to meditate and think, what they are really saying is:
I don't wish to be still and quiet my thoughts.

Shade - Relief - Comfort

Never be so quick to cut down trees or anything that gives you shade, relief and comfort.

Part Three

Short Essays

Loving Fully

Mankind is unable to love completely and totally with an agape sense of wonder. Who or what is to blame? Everyone and everything in our surrounding existence, because the "all" directly affects the "one."

Transformation is the task of every man. It is the work of Love and Love alone. Unless this metamorphosis occurs within the soul, there is no chance of change.

How must this revision come about? Through a transfusion of pondering and contemplation, self-consultation and reasoning, plus meditation do we allow the shift of thought to become alive.

One must also allow the feminine aspect to come into play; for it is only through the lioness love of womankind for her young does one understand the true meaning of "Loving Fully."

I'm Sorry - Just Two Words

These two words uttered to absolve and pardon are overused by one and all. Are we exempt and vindicated from guilt by simply saying, "I'm sorry?"

Dictionary says sorry means full of pity, deplorable and wretched. Do you feel this when expressing these two words? Are there other words that could be voiced in place of "I'm sorry"? How about I apologize, excuse me, pardon me? It's a matter of changing symbolization.

Do a little self-consultation. Let your current thought develop into using the correct inflected form of speech.

It only takes two weeks to change or form a habit. Contemplate on not only how you feel about new phrasing, but on watching people's reaction to new expressions.

The element of surprise will bring joy to your heart. And so it is.

Ten Questions

When is enough enough?
When is too much too much?
When should we speak out loud?
When should we quell our thoughts?
When is the time to fight?
When is the time to be still?
When will there be some Peace?
When will we stop fighting wars?
When will our air be pure?
When will we prize Mother Earth?

Ten questions to weigh,
Three answers to ponder. . .

1. When I, alone, feel no fear
2. When I, alone, feel no mistrust
3. When I, alone, feel God's Love

Only then will we understand "Oneness." Change happens, one act at a time.

Gift Giving

The greatest gifts are non-material. However, how do you equalize your gift giving? Is it up to par? How much did it cost? Will it be enough?

Is our gift payment or obligation? Perhaps it's time to rethink its purpose. What is the intent? Does it give tribute? Does it touch the heart?

The angels are listening to your alms. Here are a few suggestions for giving. . .
A bouquet of thank you's
A hug full of Love
A song of remembrance

Is the season of giving once a year?
"I think not," say the wisest of souls.
Listen to loved ones
Set others before oneself
Be sure the receiver feels joy.

Want/Need

What is the contrast between these two words?
How do we isolate the difference?
Need is required, a lack of, or a claim.
Want is desire, craving or wish.

I "need" food, rest and a place to call home.
Without this big three I'm long lost.
There is a brain-drain, bereavement, and destruction.
I am deprived, cut off, and disposed.

In Contrast
I "want" new shoes, jewelry and clothes.
I'm missing out on some hopes, dreams, and craves.
Yearning is taking first place as I "want"
These things in "my space."

What is your preference. . . want or need?
Contented balance should be the key.
There is room for both in a world of good deeds.
Self-centered be gone.
    Think reasons
        Be free.

Love

What is Love? Interrogation and interpretation of meaning - vital. Are we talking desire, adoration, benevolence, or heart attachment? The wonder of agape flame enables us to stand in awe of. Breathless full of surprise describes feelings of becoming enamored.

So, exactly what is Love? It is all of the above.
The heart is full of tenderness and endearment. Keeping company with pleasure is the spark that ignites passion.

Love has a multitude of layers along with fondness, admiration, revere, feel attachment for, and brother-sister, and parental affection.

If God is Love, then we must also be the same tiny bits of stardust, designed and hidden within these unimaginable coverings.

Love is whole, all, everything we need, the Alpha and Omega. This elusive intangible quality is one to hold dear. It is all the companionship we need.

Sound Travel

Does sound move as a ring in circular motion?
Does it hover, zig-zag, move vertically or drift?
Sound is energy transmitted by pressure waves.
It's utterance is supersonic.

The supernatural miraculous cadence is resounding even though sometimes unheard.
Does the directional compass point the way?
Method of voyage, superhuman.

Scientists claim we have to know the answers.
Leave no stone unturned till understanding is reached. Through soundwaves, testing and research, solutions resolve.
Would this serve mankind, womankind too?

What happened to mystery, symphony of the spheres?
Traversing through dimensions is unreal for us.
Are we meant to comprehend the puzzles of sound? Would we travel to learn how mystery works?
    Could we?
        Should we?
            Your Choice to Decide

When Will We See?

How long will it take before people actually "see?"
We live in a world blinded by comforts of materialism, no longer concerned as to how we have come to this place of existence.

The silent majority has feet of clay. They have allowed others the privilege of making decisions that directly affect their lives with no opposition from the common man.

Keeping up with the Jones' has become the norm. The ability to see into a situation, asking "why?" has been replaced with objective reality. How long can man continue to exist in a world where he cannot "see" what is happening around him.

Our creature comforts are number one, no matter how we have arrived at this fate.

Today it seems to be all about instant gratification. How sad.

A Few Gentle Moments

A few gentle moments have filled my heart with joy...

Watching my child smile as she graduated from kindergarten.

Watching my daughter's face light up as she sat in the lobby of a hotel in Athens, Greece, hoping to catch a glance from the handsome young man that served us our breakfast in the hotel cafe.

Having a tea party with my granddaughter.

Hearing my grandson tell his mom as they headed out for football practice, "Yes, we do have time. I'm going across the street to help my grammie because she needs me."

Spending an afternoon painting clouds and mountains with my precious Ellie.

Traveling to Paris and Greece with my dear friend.
What marvelous memories.

Spending an afternoon sitting in the shade of a big old tree, then enjoying pumpkin soup with a friend.

Hearing a friend's voice as she calls me every day to see if I am doing ok.
When I fell fracturing my hip, a young man rushed to my aid saying, "Everything will be alright. Hold my hand. I will pray and stay with you."

There are many more moments. Would I trade these times for say-A bag of jewels? A million dollars?

I must remember <u>not</u> to become a "muzunga" for they are ones who wander aimlessly until they end up in circles. (I read that in a book called "The Old Drift.")

I would not trade my gentle moments for anything material. This present incarnation is the only memory I have. The only things traveling with me when the time comes to shake off this body suit that is wearing out day by day are the memories of the gentle moments I have been privileged to encounter this time around.

They are priceless treasures of "Love."

Seven Challenges

Do electrons or elementary particles spin in two different directions?
Is there a parallel universe where there exists another you?
Do things appear the same in the dark as they do in the light?
Do we get to choose into which universe we reside?
Is all of this free will or do we even have a choice?
Are we split in two different versions?
Is this all there is or do we have another chance in some other alternate existence?

These seven questions can only be answered by the way I interpret them according to my individual belief. Answers cannot be proved. All depends on conceptions or consequences. Is everything dark or light? Black or White? Right or wrong?

Use your intelligence.
Be able to proceed in new directions of thought. Trust yourself.
Answers will come.

Three Stages

Would you rather catch a passel of fish, clean and scale them, or give them away to somebody?
One requires anticipation.
One requires physical exertion.
One requires letting go and giving something away.
The three stages of life being youth, middle age, and the golden age of octogenarians all exercise these same choices.

Being a member of stage number three, I find joy in giving away. I guess the old saying of "The only thing greater than anticipation is realization" is really the truth.
I have known the thrill of looking forward to something glorious. Now I am experiencing satisfaction in giving, and hopefully fulfilling, a need of another.

What a glorious ride this has been.

Shirley Taylor

Shirley is a native Idahoan. She received a Bachelor of Arts degree from Idaho State University in Elementary Education with minors in History and Music.

Her life has been spent teaching second grade, teaching piano, painting in oil and acrylics and writing...writing...writing.

Shirley's art has been displayed throughout Idaho. In 1985 at the National Governors Conference held in Boise, Idaho, her 53 oil paintings depicting Idaho scenes were presented to the fifty governors of the United States plus three territorial governors. She has been commissioned by National Frito-Lay for several projects.

This is Shirley's second book to be published.

www.ingramcontent.com/pod-product-compliance
Lightning Source LLC
Chambersburg PA
CBHW080457240426
43673CB00005B/213